120
Japanese Prints
CD-ROM and Book

Hokusai, Hiroshige and Others

Dover Publications, Inc.
Mineola, New York

The CD-ROM in this book contains all of the images. Each image is offered in two sizes on the CD—approximately 3" wide, and approximately 7" wide. Each image has been scanned at 300 dpi and saved in high-quality JPEG format. There is no installation necessary. Just insert the CD into your computer and call the images into your favorite software (refer to the documentation with your software for further instructions).

Within the Images folder on the CD, you will find two additional folders—"Large JPG" and "JPG. " Every image has a unique file name in the following format: xxx.JPG. The first 3 digits of the file name, before the period, correspond to the number printed under the image in the book. The last 3 characters of the file name, "JPG," refer to the file format. So, 001.JPG would be the first file in the folder.

Also included on the CD-ROM is Dover Design Manager, a simple graphics editing program for Windows that will allow you to view, print, crop, and rotate the images.

For technical support, contact:
Telephone: 1 (617) 249-0245
Fax: 1 (617) 249-0245
Email: dover@artimaging.com
Internet: **http://www.dovertechsupport.com**
The fastest way to receive technical support is via email or the Internet.

Bibliographical Note

120 Japanese Prints CD-ROM and Book is a new work, first published by Dover Publications, Inc., in 2006.

Dover Full-Color Electronic Design Series®

International Standard Book Number: 0-486-99740-5

Manufactured in the United States of America
Dover Publications, Inc., 31 East 2nd Street, Mineola, N.Y. 11501

002 Kiyonobu I
The Actor Ogino Sawanojō as a Woman Traveling, c. 1700–04

001 Chinchō
A Traveling Nun as Tokiwa Gozen at Fushimi, c. 1684–88

004 Toshinobu
Types from Kyoto, Edo and Osake, c. 1716–36

003 Toshinobu
Young Lovers by Mt. Fuji, c. 1720

006 Style of Moromasa
Parading Courtesan with Attendants, 1740s

005 Kiyomasu II
*The Actors Ichikawa Danzo as Soga no Goro and
Otani Hiroji as Asahina Saburo, c. 1717*

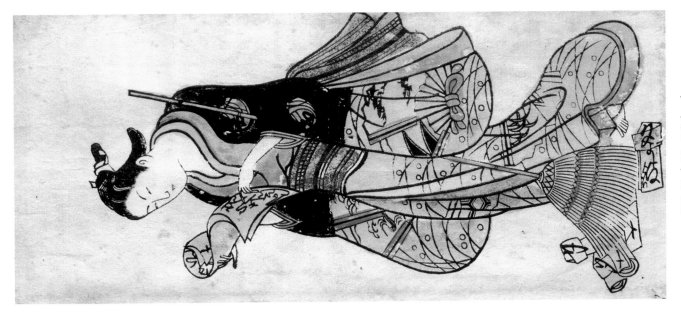

008 Early Torii School
A Beauty Reading a Letter, c. 1730

007 Early Torii School
The Kabuki Actors Sawamura Sōjūrō I and Segawa Kikunojō I, c. 1730

009 Terushige
Young Lovers Sitting at a Kotatsu, c. 1720

010 Toyonobu
Drinking Sake in a Pleasure House, n.d.

012 Kiyonobu II

Kabuki Scene of a Young Hero Battling with Two Warriors, 1752

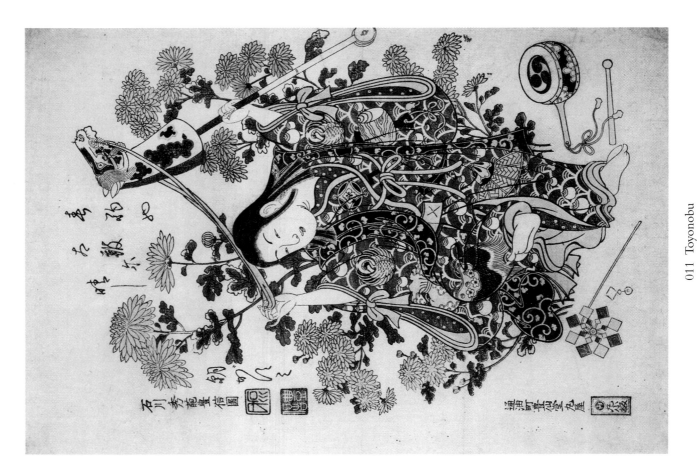

011 Toyonobu

The Young Actor Bandō Kikumatsu with a Hobby-horse, c. 1751–64

014 Kiyohiro
The Actors Yamashita Matatarō and Nakamura Tomijurō, 1755

013 Mangetsudō
Dreaming of Aubergines, c. 1744–48

016 Masanobu
The New Year's First Playing, 1755

015 Kiyohiro
The Warrior Hero Minamoto no Yoshitsune, late 1750s

018 Harunobu
Returning Sails at Shinagawa, 1764–70

017 Harunobu
A Courtesan and Attendant on a Moonlit Veranda, late 1760s

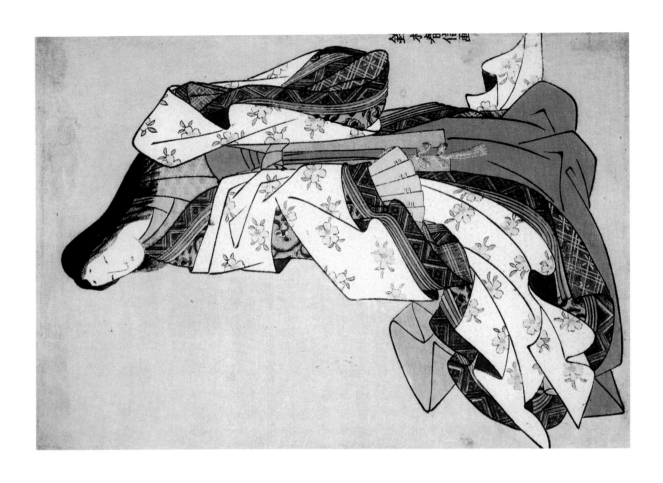

020 Harunobu
The Poetess Ono no Komachi, 1764–70

019 Harunobu
The Eirakuan Tea-house, 1764–70

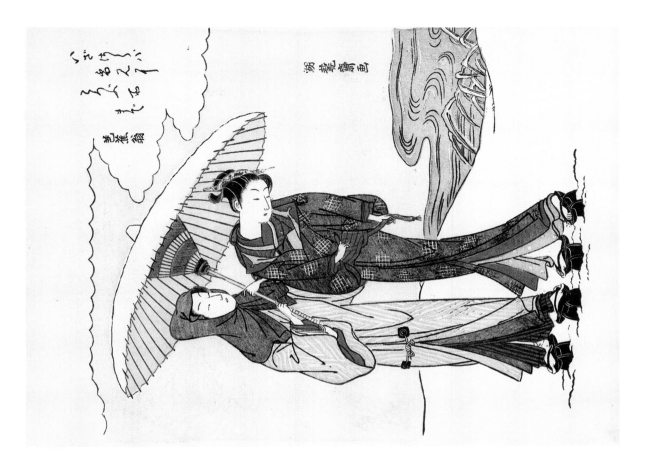

022 Koryūsai
Lovers Under an Umbrella, c. 1770s

021 Harunobu
Plum-Blossom Viewing at Night, c. late 1760s

024 Shunshō
The Actor Segawa Kikunojo II as Sagi Musume, the Heron Girl
in the Play, Meto-giku Idzu no Kisewata, c. 1770s

023 Koryūsai
The Courtesan Hanaogi with Attendants, mid 1770s

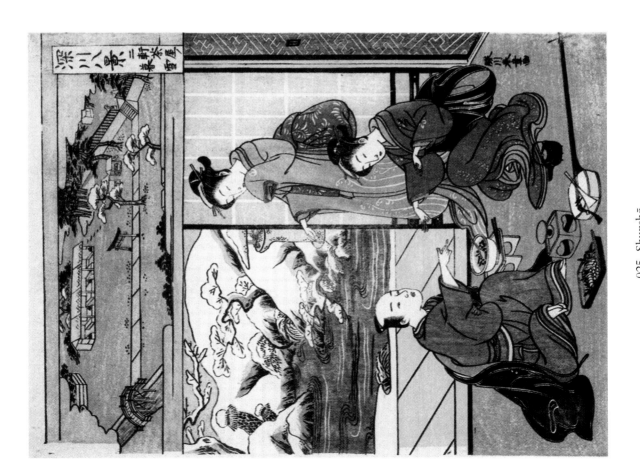

026 Shunshō
The Actors Matsumoto Kōshirō IV and Segawa Kikunojō III, c. 1780

025 Shunshō
Lingering Snow at the Niken Tea-house, c. 1772

028 Kōkan
Travesty of Ono no Komachi Praying for Rain, 1771–72

027 Shunshō
Yamauba and a Monkey, c. 1791–92

029 Toyoharu
Boating and Fireworks on the Sumida River, 1770s

030 Toyoharu
View of Mimeguri, c. 1780

032 Kiyonaga
Ferry Boat on the Sumida River, c.1780s

031 Kiyonaga
A Comparison of the Charms of Fascinating Women, c. 1780s

034 Shunchō
Autumn Excursion During an Abundant Harvest, 1770–90

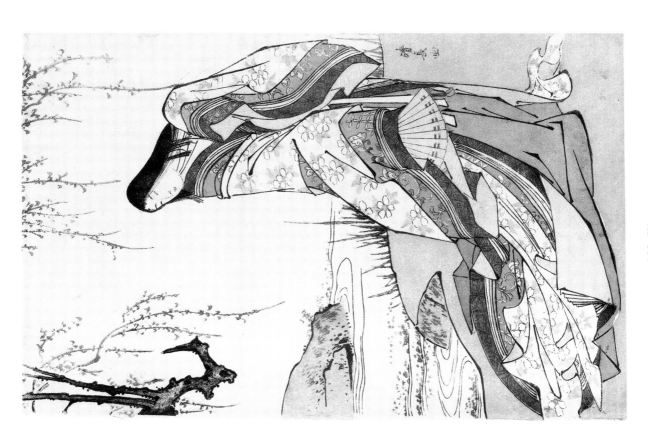

033 Kiyonaga
Portrait of Ono no Komachi, late 1700s

036 Utamaro
The Hour of the Monkey, c. 1780–1800

035 Shunchō
The Courtesan Hanaōgi, c. 1790

037 Utamaro
Colors and Scents of Flowers of the Four Seasons, c. 1784

038 Utamaro
Going Down to the East, 1795–1800

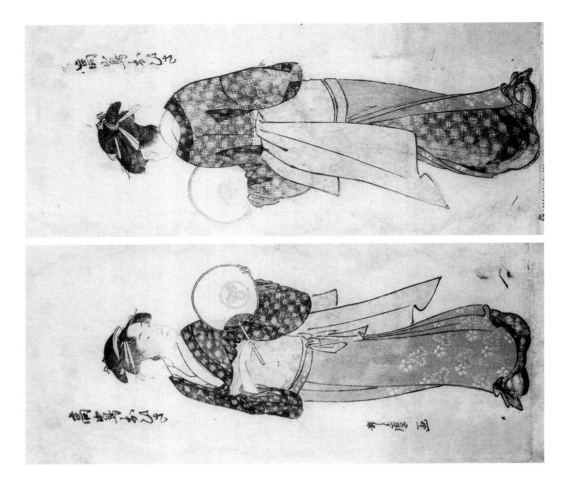

040 Utamaro
Front and Back Views of Ohisa, c. 1792

039 Utamaro
Insects and Flowers, 1788

042 Utamaro
The Fickle Type, c. 1792–93

041 Utamaro
The Beauty Ohisa, c. 1792–93

044 Utamaro
Drawing Water for Breakfast, 1795–1800

043 Utamaro
Three Beauties, mid 1790s

046 Utamaro
The Prim Type, early 1800s

045 Utamaro
Summer Bath, early 1800s

048 Gokyō
Courtesans on Promenade at New Year, late 1780s

047 Shunkō
The Kabuki Actors Ichikawa Monnosuke II and Sakata Hangorō III, mid 1780s

050 Sharaku
The Actors Nakajima Wadaemon and Nakamura Konozō, 1794

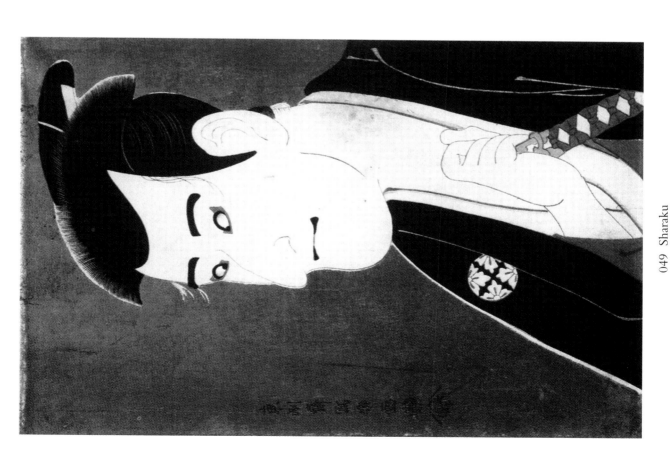

049 Sharaku
The Actor Ichikawa Komazō II as Shiga Daishichi, 1794

052 Chōki
Catching Fireflies, c. 1795

051 Sharaku
The Actor Morita Kanya, 1794

054 Chōki
New Year Sunrise, c. 1795

053 Chōki
The Courtesan Somensosuke with an Apprentice, c. 1795

056 Eishi
*Kiyomori's Daughter Painting a Self-Portrait to
Send to Her Mother*, late 1790s

055 Chōki
*Comparisons of Customs of the Eastern Capital at the Five
Annual Festivals—New Years*, c. early 1800s

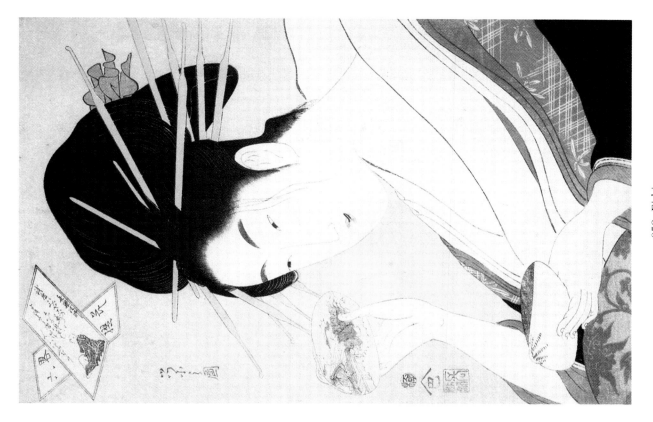

058 Eishi
A Poem by Kisen Hōshi, c. 1795–1800

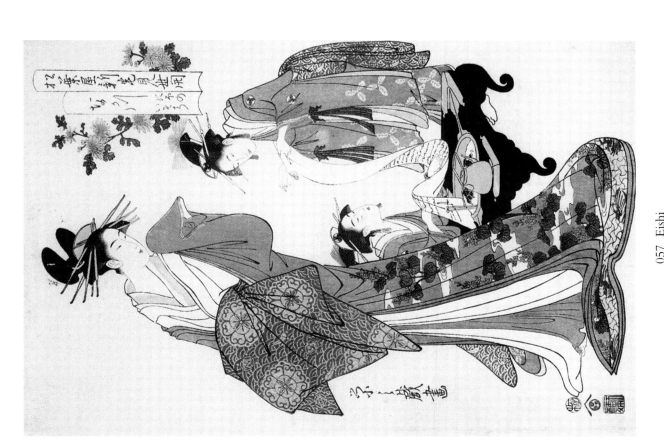

057 Eishi
The Courtesan Nakagawa with Two Apprentices, c. 1795

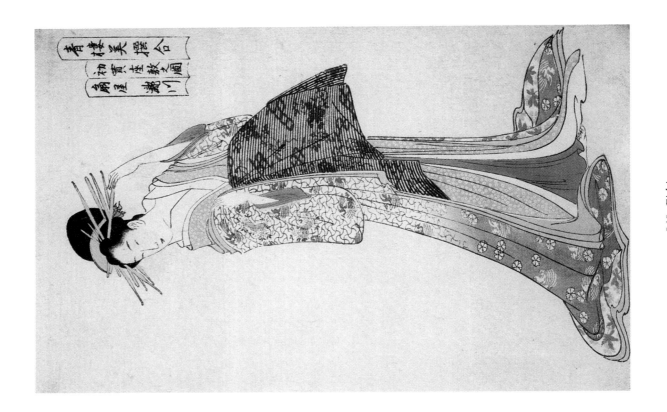

060 Eishi
The Courtesan Takikawa, c. 1796–97

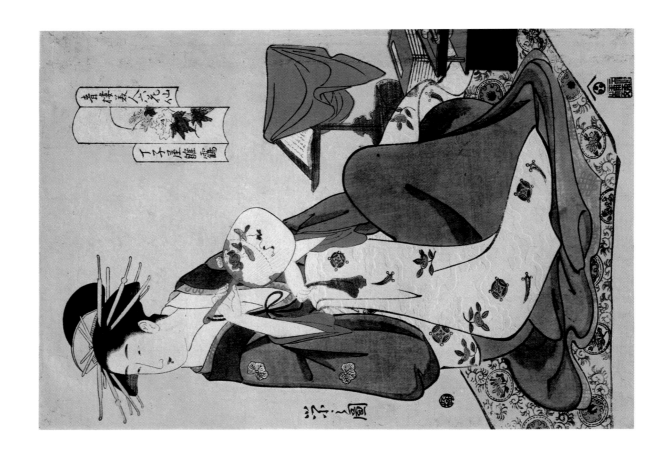

059 Eishi
The Courtesan Hinazuru of Choji-ya, c. mid 1790s

062 Eishō
The Courtesan Yosooi, late 1790s

061 Eishi
Bride and Young Girl, n.d.

064 Toyokuni
The Kabuki Actor Ichikawa Omezō I in the Drama Shibaraku, c. 1810

063 Toyokuni
The Kabuki Actor Onoe Matsusuke I, c. 1799

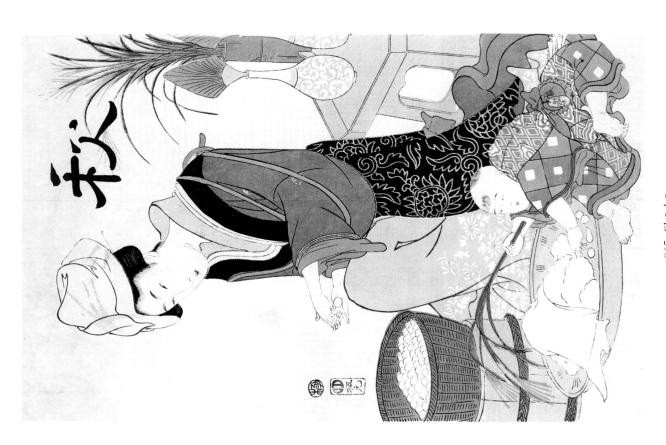

066 Toyohiro
Geisha Standing in the Wind, c. 1805

065 Shūchō
Moon Viewing in Autumn, n.d.

068 Eizan
Snow, c. late 1800s

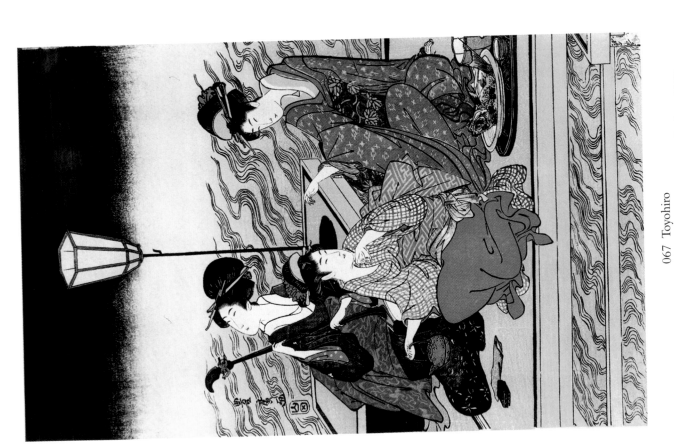

067 Toyohiro
Enjoying the Cool of the Evening at the Shijo River Bank, c. 1800s

070 Eizan
Woman at a Mirror, c. 1820

069 Eizan
The Jōruri Character Ohan with a Doll, c. 1810

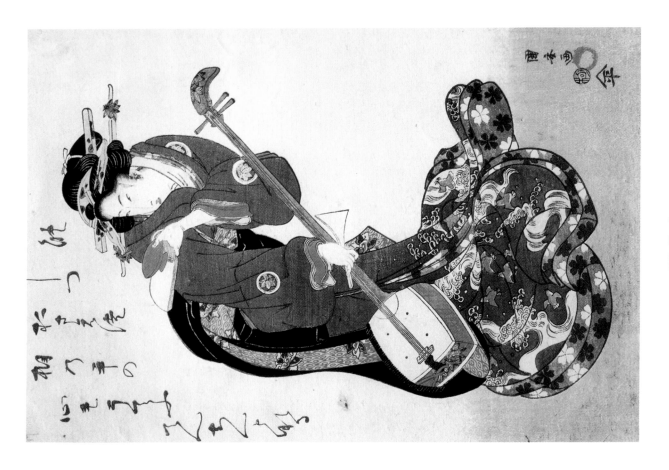

072 Kuniyasu
Geisha with Samisen, mid to late 1810s

071 Shunsen
Parading Courtesan, c. 1810

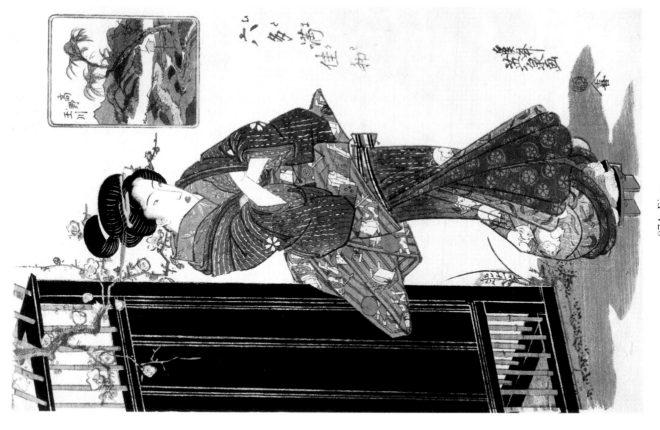

074 Eisen
The Kōya-Tama River, early 1820s

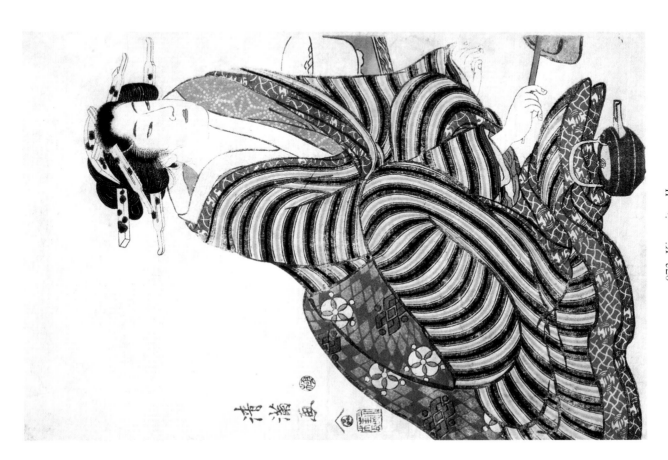

073 Kiyomitsu II
The Angry Drinker, late 1810s

076 Eisen
Geisha Girl in Eastern Capital, c. late 1820s

075 Eisen
Geisha with Samisen, early 1820s

078 Hokusai
A Rider in the Snow, c. 1833–34

077 Hokusai
Shirabyōshi Dancer, c. 1820

079 Hokusai
Thunderstorm Beneath the Summit, 1830–32

080 Hokusai
Beneath the Wave off Kanagawa, 1830–32

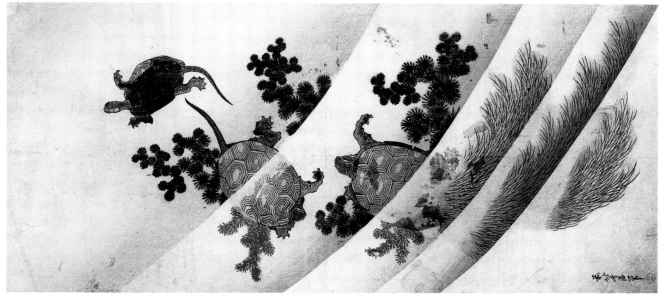

082 Hokusai
Swimming Turtles, 1832–33

081 Hokusai
Cranes on a Pine Tree, 1832–33

083 Hokusai
Peonies and Butterfly, 1833–34

084 Hokusai
Hibiscus and Sparrow, 1833–34

086 Hokusai
Kingfisher with Irises and Wild Pinks, c. 1834

085 Hokusai
Weeping Cherry and Bullfinch, c. 1834

087 Hokusai
Samurai on Horseback, 1826

088 Hokusai
The Hanging-cloud Bridge at Mount Gyōdō near Ashikaga, c. 1834

089 Hokusai
Lilies, 1832–34

090 Hokusai
Poppies, c.1834–35

091 Hokusai
Travelers Climbing a Mountain Path, c. 1835–36

092 Hokusai
Women Returning Home at Sunset, c. 1835–36

093 Hokusai
Nakamaro Watching the Moon from a Hill, c. 1835–36

094 Hokusai
Old Tiger in the Snow, 1849

096 Hokushū
The Kabuki Actor Nakamura Utaemon III in the Role of a Samurai, 1825

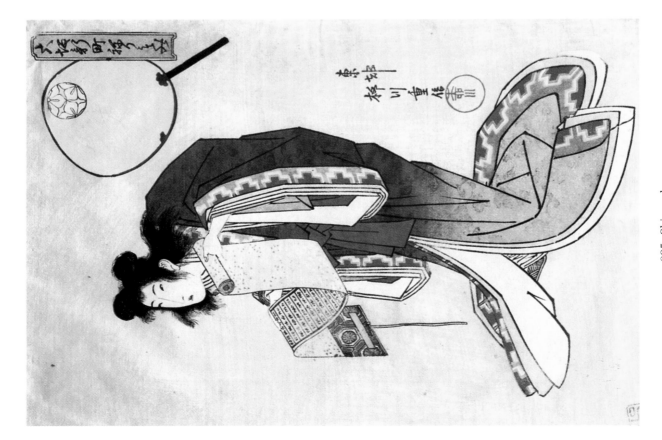

095 Shigenobu
The Courtesan Manju-dayū as a Processional Figure, 1822

098 Kunisada
Geisha Wiping her Face, late 1820s

097 Kunisada
The Teahouse at Edo, c. 1827

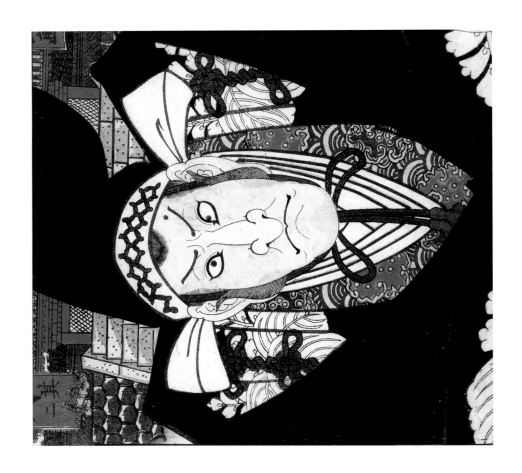

100 Kunisada
Moronao, the Villain of the Kabuki Play Chushingura, 1852

099 Kunisada
A Horse under a Willow, 1830s

102 Hiroshige
Double-Petaled Cherry Blossoms and Small Bird, c. 1830s

101 Hiroshige
Peonies, n.d.

103 Hiroshige
Crossing at Suda, c. 1830s

104 Hiroshige
Hakone—View of the Lake, 1831–34

105 Hiroshige
Evening Cherry at Nakanochō in the Yoshiwara, c. 1834–35

106 Hiroshige
Men Poling Boats Past a Bank with Willows, c. 1834–42

107 Hiroshige
Crane and Wave, mid 1830s

108 Hiroshige
Sunrise on New Year's Day at Susaki, mid 1830s

109 Hiroshige
Two Ladies Conversing in the Snow, 1853

110 Hiroshige
The Pine Beach at Miho in Suruga Province, 1853–56

112 Hiroshige

111 Hiroshige

114 Hiroshige
Woman on a River Bank in the Evening, 1856–58

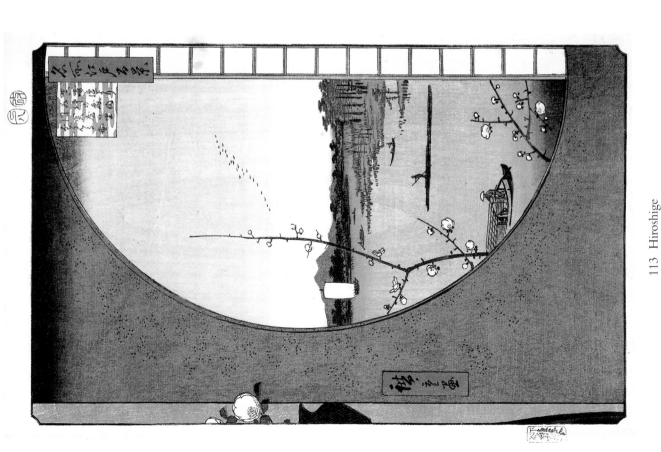

113 Hiroshige
*A View from near Massaki of Suijin Shrine, Uchikawa
River and the Village of Sekiya, 1856–58*

116 Hokuei

115 Hiroshige

118 Kuniyoshi
View of Mt. Fuji on a Clear Day from off Tsukuda, c. 1843

119 Kuniyoshi
Distant View of Mt. Fuji from Shōhei Hill, c. 1843

120 Yoshitoshi

ALPHABETICAL LIST OF ARTISTS

Chinchō 001

Chōki. 052–055

Eisen 074–076

Eishi 056–061

Eishō 062

Eizan 068–070

Gokyō 048

Harunobu 017–021

Hiroshige 101–115

Hokuei 116

Hokusai. 077–094

Hokushū 096

Kiyohiro 014–015

Kiyomasu II 005

Kiyonaga 031–033

Kiyonobu I 002

Kiyonobu II 012

Kōkan. 028

Koryūsai 022–023

Kunimasu. 117

Kunisada 097–100

Kuniyasu 072

Kuniyoshi. 118–119

Kiyomitsu II 073

Mangetsudō. 013

Masanobu 016

Moromasa, style of 006

Sharaku 049–051

Shigenobu 095

Shūchō 065

Shunchō 034–035

Shunkō 047

Shunsen. 071

Shunshō. 024–027

Terushige 009

Torii, early school 007–008

Toshinobu 003–004

Toyoharu 029–030

Toyohiro 066–067

Toyokuni 063–064

Toyonobu. 010–011

Utamaro 036–046

Yoshitoshi. 120